# The African Americans

## RICHARD BOWEN

# MAJOR AMERICAN IMMIGRATION

MASON CREST PUBLISHERS • PHILADELPHIA

Dr. Martin Luther King Jr. speaks to a large crowd from the steps of the Lincoln Memorial in August 1963. The March on Washington was an important moment in the history of African-American civil rights in the United States.

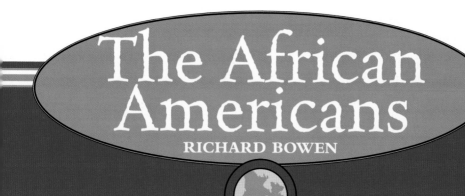

# The African Americans

## RICHARD BOWEN

# MAJOR AMERICAN IMMIGRATION

MASON CREST PUBLISHERS • PHILADELPHIA

Mason Crest Publishers
370 Reed Road
Broomall PA 19008
www.masoncrest.com

First printing

1 3 5 7 9 8 6 4 2


Library of Congress Cataloging-in-Publication Data

Bowen, Richard.
  The African Americans / Richard Bowen.
      p. cm. — (Major American immigration)
  Includes bibliographical references and index.
  ISBN-13: 978-1-4222-0603-4 (hardcover)
  ISBN-10: 1-4222-0603-3 (hardcover)
  ISBN-13: 978-1-4222-0670-6 (pbk.)
  ISBN-10: 1-4222-0670-X (pbk.)
  1. African Americans—History—Juvenile literature. I. Title.
  E185.M69 2008
  973'.0496073—dc22
                                                    2008026018

## Table of Contents

# MAJOR AMERICAN IMMIGRATION

## America's Ethnic Heritage

**Barry Moreno, librarian**
**Statue of Liberty/**
**Ellis Island National Monument**

**E**thnic diversity is one of the most striking characteristics of the American identity. In the United States the Bureau of the Census officially recognizes 122 different ethnic groups. North America's population had grown by leaps and bounds, starting with the American Indian tribes and nations—the continent's original people—and increasing with the arrival of the European colonial migrants who came to these shores during the 16th and 17th centuries. Since then, millions of immigrants have come to America from every corner of the world.

But the passage of generations and the great distance of America from the "Old World"—Europe, Africa, and Asia—has in some cases separated immigrant peoples from their roots. The struggle to succeed in America made it easy to forget past traditions. Further, the American spirit of freedom, individualism, and equality gave Americans a perspective quite different from the view of life shared by residents of the Old World.

Immigrants of the 19th and 20th centuries recognized this at once. Many tried to "Americanize" themselves by tossing away their peasant clothes and dressing American-style even before reaching their new homes in the cities or the countryside of America. It was not so easy to become part of America's culture, however. For many immigrants, learning English was quite a hurdle. In fact, most older immigrants clung to the old ways, preferring to speak their native languages and follow their familiar customs and traditions. This was easy to do when ethnic neighborhoods abounded in large North American cities like New York, Montreal, Philadelphia, Chicago, Toronto, Boston, Cleveland, St. Louis, New Orleans and San Francisco. In rural areas, farm families—many of them Scandinavian, German, or Czech—established their own tightly knit communities. Thus foreign languages and dialects, religious beliefs, Old World customs, and certain class distinctions flourished.

The most striking changes occurred among the children of immigrants, whose hopes and dreams were different from those of their parents. They began breaking away from the Old World customs, perhaps as a reaction to the embarrassment of being labeled "foreigner." They badly wanted to be Americans, and assimilated more easily than their parents and grandparents. They learned to speak English without a foreign accent, to dress and act like other Americans. The assimilation of the children of immigrants was encouraged by social contact—games, schools, jobs, and military service—which further broke down the barriers between immigrant groups and hastened the process of Americanization. Along the way, many family traditions were lost or abandoned.

Today, the pride that Americans have in their ethnic roots is one of the abiding strengths of both the United States and Canada. It shows that the theory which called America a "melting pot" of the world's people was never really true. The thought that a single "American" would emerge from the combination of these peoples has never happened, for Americans have grown more reluctant than ever before to forget the struggles of their ethnic forefathers. The growth of cultural studies and genealogical research indicates that Americans are anxious not to entirely lose this identity, whether it is English, French, Chinese, African, Mexican, or some other group. There is an interest in tracing back the family line as far as records or memory will take them. In a sense, this has made Americans a divided people; proud to be Americans, but proud also of their ethnic roots.

As a result, many Americans have welcomed a new identity, that of the hyphenated American. This unique description has grown in usage over the years and continues to grow as more Americans recognize the importance of family heritage. In the end, this is an appreciation of America's great cultural heritage and its richness of its variety.

"Cotton Fields in the Deep South," a painting by the American artist William A. Walker, shows African slaves at work picking cotton on a large plantation. Walker was interested in the plight of the slaves; some of his other paintings appear on pp. 15, 34, and 38 of this book.

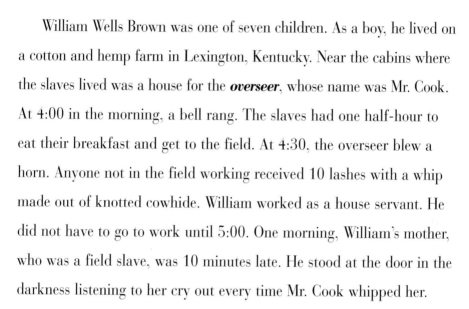

# 1 The Story of William Wells Brown

William Wells Brown was one of seven children. As a boy, he lived on a cotton and hemp farm in Lexington, Kentucky. Near the cabins where the slaves lived was a house for the **overseer**, whose name was Mr. Cook. At 4:00 in the morning, a bell rang. The slaves had one half-hour to eat their breakfast and get to the field. At 4:30, the overseer blew a horn. Anyone not in the field working received 10 lashes with a whip made out of knotted cowhide. William worked as a house servant. He did not have to go to work until 5:00. One morning, William's mother, who was a field slave, was 10 minutes late. He stood at the door in the darkness listening to her cry out every time Mr. Cook whipped her.

William's owner later bought a farm near St. Louis, Missouri. His owner often hired him out to others, which meant people paid the owner for William's work. Around St. Louis, William worked for a number of cruel and heartless people. He said, "Though slavery is thought by some to be mild in Missouri, when compared with the cotton, sugar, and rice growing states, yet no part of our…country [was] more noted for the [cruelty] of its inhabitants than St. Louis." William knew many African Americans who had been beaten severely. He knew of one woman who was beaten to death and a man who was burned alive.

For a while, William was employed by Elijah P. Lovejoy, the editor and publisher of the *St. Louis Observer* newspaper. William said, "My work while with him was mainly in the printing office, waiting on hands, working the press, etc. Mr. Lovejoy was a very good man. I am chiefly indebted to him, and to my employment in the printing office, for what little learning I obtained in slavery."

Another time, William worked as a waiter on a steamboat. The job was pleasant, and the man he worked for was not cruel. As he worked, he saw the faces of people who were free, who could come and go as they pleased. He thought of escaping and going to Canada, where he heard slaves could live free and were protected. But he would then think of his mother, who was still working as a field slave. He vowed he would not leave the land of slavery without her.

**Elijah P. Lovejoy often wrote in favor of the abolition of slavery. Protesters eventually forced him to move to Alton, Illinois, where he became editor of the *Alton Observer*. At the age of 35, Lovejoy was killed for his abolitionist views by an angry mob.**

William also worked as a "soul driver." This meant he watched over gangs of slaves that were being transported in chains to places where they could be sold. William said, "I was heartsick at seeing my fellow creatures bought and sold." With William leading them, the gangs of 50 or 60 men and women first traveled on foot. Then they boarded a steamboat. After journeying a few days on the water, they arrived at the city or town where they were to be auctioned. They were kept in an open-air "pen" where prospective buyers would

**A slave family outside their home in the mid-19th century.**

come and view them. "On auction day," William said, "it was not uncommon...to pass by an auction stand, and behold a woman upon the auction block, and hear the seller crying out, 'How much is offered for this woman? She is a good cook, good washer, a good obedient servant. She has got religion!'" Buyers often separated small children from their mothers.

Once William went to see his sister, who had been sold to a man along with four other women. He said, "She was seated with her face towards the door where I entered, yet she did not look up until I walked up to her. As soon as she observed me, she sprung up and threw her arms around my neck, leaned her head upon my breast, and, without uttering a word, bust into tears. She advised me to take mother and try to get out of slavery. She said there was no hope for herself—that she must live and die a slave. After giving her some advice and taking from my finger a ring and placing it upon hers, I bade her farewell forever....Then and there I made up my mind to leave for Canada as soon as possible."

William's mother did not want to try to escape. She told him that since all her children were in slavery, she did not want to leave them. William persuaded her to join him, however. He had saved some money from doing errands. With this, he bought crackers, cheese, and dried beef. When he met his mother, she put these in a sack. At 9:00 at night, they left St. Louis in a small boat and paddled across the Mississippi River to Illinois. They knew their masters would be looking for them, so they hid in the woods during the day. At night, they traveled in the darkness, using the North Star as their guide. William wrote, "As we traveled towards [Canada], my heart would at times leap for joy. At other times, being as I was almost constantly on my feet, I felt as though I could travel no further. But when I thought of ...the prospect of liberty before me, I was encouraged to press forward, my heart was strengthened, and I forgot I was tired and hungry."

On the tenth day of their travels, William and his mother ran out of food and were soaking wet from heavy rains that had fallen. They decided to ask for something to eat at a farmhouse. The people at the house treated them with kindness and advised them to continue to travel at night. A few days later, three men on horseback suddenly rode up to them. As they dismounted, William asked them what they wanted. One of the men took out a poster that advertised a $200 reward for their capture and return to St. Louis.

They tied William's hands and then took them to a house, where they spent the night. The next day, a blacksmith came and put handcuffs on William. Four days later, they were back in St. Louis. "I cannot describe my feelings upon approaching the city," William remembered.

This William Walker painting from 1850 shows a slave cabin. Trusted slaves were given their own homes where they could live with their families. Most of the workers had to live in crowded bunkhouses.

THE PARTING "Buy us too."

They were locked into jail. The man who owned William's mother said he would sell her to a slave trader in New Orleans. A week later, William arrived back at his owner's house. His owner, whose name was Mr. Young, sent William to work in the field, where the overseer gave him a severe beating. A short time later, Mr. Young sold William to a man named Mr. Willi.

William arranged to see his mother on the boat that would be carrying her to New Orleans. William said, "I went on board...the boat, and found her in company with 50 or 60 other slaves. She was chained to another woman. Seeing me, she immediately dropped her head....She moved not, neither did she weep. Her emotion was too deep for tears. I approached, threw my arms around her neck,

Abolitionists—people who opposed slavery and wanted to see it forbidden, or abolished—often published pamphlets to stir up sympathy for African slaves. In this colored drawing from the late 1850s, a white plantation owner holds the chains of a black man he has just purchased, while the slave's wife begs the owner to buy her and their child as well so the family would not be split up.

kissed her, and fell upon my knees, begging her forgiveness, for I thought myself to blame for her sad condition; for if I had not persuaded her to accompany me, she would not then have been in chains. She finally raised her head, looked me in the face and said, 'My dear son, you are not to blame for my being here. You have done nothing more or less than your duty. Do not weep for me. I cannot last long upon a cotton plantation. I feel that my Heavenly Master will soon call me home, and then I shall be out of the hands of the slave-holders!'" They could see Mr. Mansfield, who owned his mother, coming toward them. She whispered into William's ear, "My child, we must soon part to meet no more on this side of the grave. You have ever said that you would not die a slave; that you would be a free man. Now try to get your liberty!" As she said this, Mansfield kicked William out of the way. His mother cried, "God be with you!" It was the last time he saw her.

While living with Mr. Willi's family, William began to make plans for his escape. Although Mr. Willi treated him better than his previous master, he remained unhappy because he was not free. Mr. Willi eventually sold William to a merchant living in St. Louis named Captain Price. His wife wanted him for a carriage driver. Mrs. Price took pride in her servants and kept them dressed well. As soon as she had William, she bought a new carriage. Mrs. Price was determined to wed William to a woman named Eliza, who was owned by a neighboring doctor. She told him she would purchase Eliza if he wanted her for his wife. William saw this as a trap to make him feel satisfied with his life with the Price family. He wanted to be on good terms with Mrs. Price, however, so that there would be no suspicion about his escape. Therefore, he promised Mrs. Price he would marry Eliza, but not right away.

The family made a trip to New Orleans in a boat they owned. William served as a *steward*. After spending some time in New Orleans, they decided to travel up the Mississippi to Cincinnati, which was a free state. William said, "The long-looked-for opportunity to make my escape from slavery was near at hand." Mr. Price was concerned about taking William to a state where he might be able to escape. He asked William if he had ever been to a free state. To reassure him, William replied, "Oh yes, I have been in Ohio. My master carried me to that state once, but I never liked a free state." Mrs. Price asked William if he still felt dearly about Eliza, whom they had brought with them on the trip. William said that he felt as if they were married already and that only death would come between them. This had the effect William desired. They felt confident William would not try to escape, and the boat proceeded up the river.

Near a small village in Ohio, William saw his opportunity. As the boat was unloading passengers and cargo, he went ashore and then walked into the woods. He had a little money with him, a suit of clothes, some food, and a tinderbox to make a fire. He remained in the woods until night, because he knew that even in Ohio he was in danger of being arrested.

After darkness fell, he came out of the woods onto the main road. Not being able to see the North Star because it was cloudy, he did not know which way to go. William recalled, "I walked up and down the road until near midnight, when the clouds disappeared, and I welcomed the sight of my friend—truly the slave's friend—the North Star! As soon as I saw it I knew my course."

On the fifth day, it rained hard, freezing as it fell. The wind blew in his face as he walked. William's clothes became a "glare of ice;" his body became numb and chilled. Finding shelter in an old barn, he said, "I...looked upon that night as the most eventful part of my escape.... Nothing but the providence of God, and that old barn kept me from freezing to death." He now had a cold and his feet were partially frost-bitten, which made it difficult to walk, but he was determined to keep going. He decided to seek help. He hid behind some brush, intending to stop someone. Soon he saw an old man walking down the road leading a white horse. When he saw him, somehow he knew the man would help. When William approached, the man asked "if [he] was not a slave." Not answering the question, William asked him if he knew anyone who might help him, since he was ill. The man replied he would, but asked him again if he was a slave. William told him he was. The man advised William to hide because he was in a very pro-slavery neighborhood. The man said he would return to him with a wagon and horses, then rode off. William was afraid he might bring someone to arrest him, so he hid a little farther away. When the man returned, he brought the wagon and horses he had promised.

The man, whose name was Wells Brown, took William to his house, where he and his wife cared for him for two weeks, and bought him clothes and a pair of boots. William said, "The fact that I was in all probability a free man, sounded in my ears like a charm. I wanted to see mother and sister, that I might tell them, 'I was free!' I wanted to see my fellow slaves in St. Louis and let them know that the chains were no longer upon my limbs. I wanted to see Captain Price, and let him learn from my own lips that I was no more a *chattel*, but a man!"

William learned he was about 150 miles from Cleveland, Ohio, on Lake Erie, which bordered Canada. Before William left to continue on his journey, Mr. Brown, who was not in good health, asked him what name he was going to take. Mr. Brown said free men always had two names. William asked him for a name, since he was the first friend he had as a free man. Mr. Brown said, "I shall call [you] Wells Brown, after myself." Thereafter, William became William Wells Brown.

With a little money that the Browns gave him, William started again for Canada. After two days, however, the money ran out. He went to the

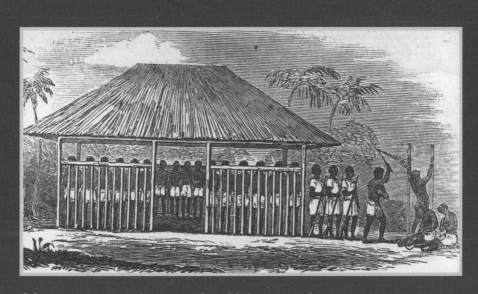

A barracoon was a large pen in which captured slaves were kept. In this engraving from about 1850, a disobedient slave is whipped in front of the pen while armed guards watch.

first farmhouse he saw and knocked on the door. A man answered, and William told him he would like some food. The man said he would not just give him anything, but that he could work for something to eat. Just then, the wife of the man came to the door and asked her husband what William wanted. The man did not want to reply. She then asked William directly, to which he replied that he wanted something to eat. She told him to come in. William walked up to the door, but the man blocked the way. The woman asked her husband to move out of the way. When he did not, she pushed him aside, and William entered. After William had eaten as much as he wanted, the woman gave him a note to introduce him to her friend down the road and 10 cents, which was all the money she had.

Three days later, William arrived in Cleveland, but because it was winter he had to remain there until spring, when the ice melted on Lake Erie, so he could sail on a boat over to Canada. Feeling that he was now out of danger, he got a job as a waiter. During this time, he also bought some books and began to educate himself. William said, "It was my great desire, being out of slavery myself, to do what I could for the *emancipation* of my brethren yet in chains, and while on Lake Erie, I found many opportunities....While on the lake, I always made arrangements to carry them on the boat to Buffalo or Detroit, and thus effect their escape to 'the promised land.'" After his escape to Canada, William Wells Brown spent many years of his life working for the freedom of American slaves. ✹

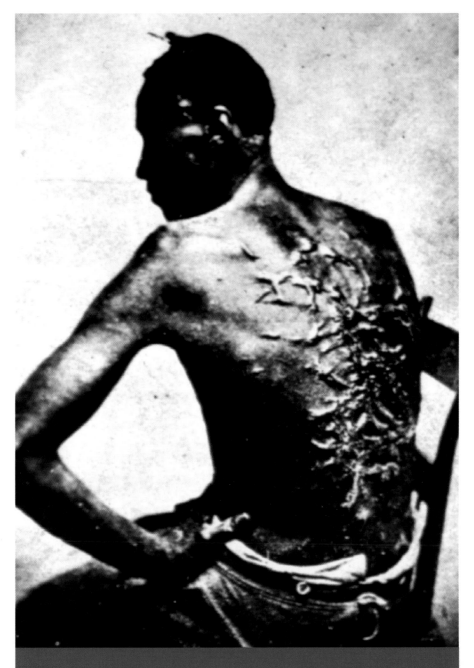

This 1863 photograph shows the scarred back of an African-American slave. The horrible scars were caused by repeated whippings.

George Washington speaks with a slave on his Mount Vernon estate in this painting. Although the Declaration of Independence, written at the start of the American Revolution, stated that "all men are created equal," many leaders of the Revolution were slaveowners. Unlike many slaveowners, however, Washington ordered his slaves to be freed after his death.

## Why Africans Came—
## The Reasons for Slavery

Economics was the primary reason slavery existed. It saved people money and effort to have others do work for them for which they did not pay them anything. A person who wanted to buy another person as a slave had to pay for that individual and furnish food, clothing, and shelter. Beyond that, any labor the slave provided and any money the slave made went to the slave owner. With slaves working a minimum of 12 hours a day, six days a week, all year long, it is easy to see that a slave owner could gain a lot of profit in time, energy, and money by owning slaves.

In the early settlement of the Americas, Native Americans were the first people to be put to work as slaves. They worked for the white people who were coming from Europe. The Europeans needed laborers to perform tasks such as mining and farming. But the Native American slaves often died working because of the extreme hardship under which they toiled. Diseases also became widespread. As their numbers began to dwindle, the people who owned farms, mines, and other businesses began to look elsewhere for slaves.

Slave traders began bringing Africans to the New World in large numbers in the 1500s. The first people to bring slaves were the Spanish. Later, the Portuguese, French, English, and Dutch joined the slave trade.

At that time, most of the African people were not organized into states or countries. Instead, they lived in small groups or tribes. This made **conflicts** among the Africans quite common. In wars between tribes, defeated warriors or captured members of another tribe were often forced to work for those who had captured them. Within the tribe, criminals or people who had large debts might also be enslaved. But these Africans still were able to marry, have property, and participate in the normal activities of the people for whom they worked as slaves in Africa. In addition, they could eventually become free by working for their freedom, or buying it. In some cases the slave owner would let them go free.

This was not the case for slaves in the New World. Most Africans who were brought to America would be slaves for life. In addition, slavery was **hereditary**, so their children would also be slaves.

In some cases, the people brought in chains to the New World had been captured by other Africans, who sold them to European slave traders. This does not mean, however, that Africans were responsible for the slave trade. The European buyers the Europeans and the sellers in Africa contributed equally to this evil business. The slave trade operated like many other businesses, but because its "trade goods" were human beings, it was a uniquely tragic activity, resulting in horrible experiences and **moral** conflicts.

The first slaves were brought to North America in 1619, when a Dutch slave trader landed at the English settlement of Jamestown.

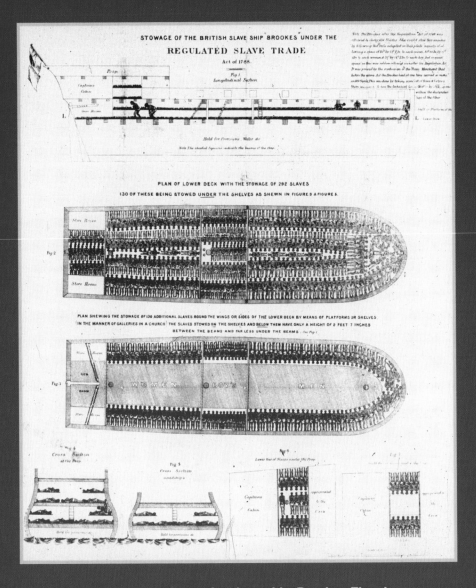

This drawing from 1788 shows the slave ship *Brookes.* The slaves were packed tightly together, with 292 loaded into the lower deck and another 130 on shelves around the edges. The slaves had less than three feet of headroom for the journey across the Atlantic Ocean, which could take three to six weeks.

# 3

## How They Came

Europeans captured Africans to make into slaves or traded for them with other Africans. Also, Africans who were trading slaves among themselves began to trade them instead to the whites. Because there were many small groups living in Africa, each with its own royalty, many of the people who were captured were of royal blood. (This was in contrast to the later European immigrants, who were often from the lower classes.) The Africans who traded slaves often traded away those with royal blood because they were more difficult to keep and refused to do manual labor. The traders exchanged human beings for money, guns, clothing, alcohol, or other items. In order to capture people, historians say whites sometimes used red or *calico* cloth, which attracted the people to their ships. Richard Jones of Union, South Carolina, said that his grandmother, who was born in Africa, used to tell him the following story:

> Granny Judith said that in Africa they had very few pretty things, and that
> they had no red colors in cloth, in fact, they had no cloth at all. Some
> strangers with pale faces come one day and draped a small piece of red
> flannel down on the ground. All the black folks grabbed for it. Then a
> larger piece was draped a little further on, and on until the river was
> reached. Then a large piece was draped in the river and on the other side.
> They was led on, each one trying to git a piece as it was draped. Finally,
> when the ship was reached, they draped large pieces on the plank and up

into the ship till they got as many blacks on board as they wanted. Then the gate was chained up, and they could not get back. That is the way Granny Judith say they got her to America.

Olaudah Equiano, who was born in 1743 near the Niger River in Africa, told the following story about being captured by Africans.

> One day, when all our people were gone out to their works as usual, and only I and my dear sister were left to mind the house, two men and a woman got over the walls, and in a moment seized us both; and without giving us time to cry out, or make resistance, they stopped our mouths and ran off with us into the nearest wood….For a long time we had kept in the woods, but at last we came into a road….I had now some hopes of being delivered; for…I discovered some people at a distance, on which I began to cry out for their assistance; but my cries had no other effect than to make them tie me faster and stop my mouth, and then they put me into a large sack.

After they were captured, the people were branded. This means a symbol was burned into their skin so that other slave traders could not steal them. Then, they were taken to forts along the ocean. From the forts, they were loaded into the holds of ships, where they were chained together with iron chains. The holds were hot, humid, and cramped. Sanitary conditions were horrible and produced many diseases, such as dysentery, smallpox, dehydration, and yellow fever. It usually required between five and eight weeks to sail over the ocean. Out of 100 slaves crossing the Atlantic, between 10 and 40 died. The more thoughtful ship captains fed the captives the foods they were used to eating, including potatoes, corn, yams, rice, and palm oil. Other slaves had to eat European food, like beef, bread, cheese, and beans. Sometimes the food ran out and the people

A European explorer named Mungo Park wrote his observations of the Africans he saw as he traveled on the Gambia River. He said, "They were all very inquisitive, but they viewed me at first with looks of horror, and repeatedly asked if my countrymen were cannibals. They were very desirous to know what became of the slaves after they had crossed the salt water. I told them that they were employed in cultivating the land, but they would not believe me; and one of them, putting his hand upon the ground said, with great simplicity, 'Have you really got such ground as this to set your feet upon?' A deeply rooted idea that the whites purchase Negroes for the purpose of devouring them, or of selling them to others, that they may be devoured hereafter, naturally makes the slaves contemplate a journey towards the coast with great terror."

Captured Africans are marched through the bush, shackled by their necks and hands. An armed overseer with a gun walks beside them. This illustration is from a book by the English missionary and explorer Dr. David Livingstone, *Narrative of the Expedition to the Zambesi.*

arrived thin and hungry. Sometimes the slave owners whipped the slaves and used mouth openers to force-feed those who refused to eat. Other torture devices used were thumbscrews and **manacles**.

At first, Africans thought those that captured their relatives and neighbors were **cannibals**. This was because after they were put on the ships, they were never seen again. (Europeans also thought the Africans practiced cannibalism.)

White people also tended to justify slavery by telling stories in which whites were superior to black people. For example, one story told by **missionaries** states:

The great God in heaven, after he had created heaven and earth, made two large chests, and placed them near the dwellings of mankind....The black people on discovering the chests, ran immediately to examine them, and found one locked and the other open. Not thinking it possible to open that which was locked, they contended themselves with the other, which they found quite full of...tools, such as hoes, axes, and spades, when each seized as much as he could carry, and all returned home. A little while after, the white people came also, and very calmly began to examine the locked chest, and knowing the way to open it, found it filled with books, and papers which they took and carried away. Upon which God said, "I perceive, that the black people mean to till the ground, and the white people to learn to read and write." The Negroes, therefore, believe, that it thus pleased the Almighty to put mankind to the proof; and as the blacks did not show as much sense as the white people, He made them subject to the latter, and decreed that they should have a troublesome life in this world.

While these stories made whites feel less guilty, they did not ease the pain Africans suffered as they were taken from their homelands, marched to the ocean shore, placed into the cramped holds of ships, and transported thousands of miles across the Atlantic Ocean with no hope of ever returning. ▣

This painting shows a cotton plantation in the American South. African slaves were needed to help the plantations operate profitably.

## 4 What They Did

By 1700, the influence of the kings and queens of Europe went far beyond the European countries themselves. Colonies were developing in the New World, and workers were needed to help make them prosperous. The Atlantic slave trade provided these workers. Agriculture was becoming big business in the colonies, especially around Chesapeake Bay and the southeastern parts of the United States. Slaves were needed to clear land. They cut and burned trees, split logs, and built fences. A young black man might become a carpenter, a *wheelwright*, or a cabinetmaker. An industry in which many Africans worked was barrel making. Barrels were essential for shipping. They held rum and fish from New England, grains and tobacco from the Chesapeake area, *indigo* and rice from South Carolina, and sugar and molasses from the West Indies. In South Carolina over several generations, Africans dug an intricate network of canals that linked local rivers for irrigation and transportation. Slaves built roads in the Chesapeake Bay area upon which large wooden *hogsheads* of tobacco were rolled.

Trade between colonies depended on ocean travel. Slaves cut pine trees for timber, and used the sap to make *tar and pitch,* used in ship maintenance. They also built ships and became sailors. Other skilled slaves were metal and leather workers, cloth makers, and *artisans*. Whites learned from Africans in many areas. For example, in the Carolinas, English colonists were unable to grow crops in large quantities. Their slaves began growing rice in the swampy areas in order to feed themselves. After the Africans taught the English how to grow and harvest the rice, many Carolina landowners became rich from the crop.

Altogether, between 10 and 12 million Africans were brought to the New World. Ninety-five percent went to South America and the Caribbean. Only 5 percent (a total of 500,000) came to North America. These people arrived between 1700 and 1807. After 1807 the United States outlawed the ***importing*** of African slaves.

Unlike the many immigrants who came to the New World full of hope for a new and better life, African slaves came facing a life of ***servitude***. This was true not only for themselves, but also for their relatives and children. Work dominated the slaves' existence, and the slave owner rigidly controlled all other parts of their lives. Arriving chained together in the dark, cramped hold of a slave ship, the African Americans must have felt terribly isolated, afraid, and hopeless.

Upon landing, slaves were often kept in a "pen" where they could be viewed by people who wanted to purchase them. They were fed well so that they would lose any appearance of mistreatment or starvation from the terrible ocean voyage, and so they would appear healthy to the buyers and therefore worth more money. After being sold, they were taken to the home of their new owner.

Black women worked in the fields. They also worked as domestic servants, cleaning house, sewing, mending, and washing clothes. Food

This is the interior of a slave pen in Alexandria, Virginia, from the 1860s. It was owned by Price, Birch and Company.

preparation meant going to the market, tending the garden, cooking, and even feeding, slaughtering, and butchering livestock. Black women had to take care of the needs of the white family that owned them in addition to their own families. It was not unusual for a slave owner to order a black woman to stop feeding her own child in order to care for the white children.

William A. Walker painted this scene of two cotton pickers around 1850.

Black males worked in the fields and performed other work on the plantation, such as digging ditches and clearing land. In addition, males often worked off the plantation as lumberjacks, salt, coal, or gold miners, or textile workers. The money that slaves earned went directly to their owners.

Both men and women worked as house servants, where the work was perhaps easier than that of the field hands. House servants, however, had to take care of the slightest wish of any member of the white family. They were also subject to abuse, including sexual assault.

In the years prior to the American Civil War, agriculture was big business that promoted the expansion of slavery. The invention of the

## THE SLAVE REVOLTS OF DENMARK VESEY AND NAT TURNER

Denmark Vesey was an African-American carpenter who had freed himself and become fairly wealthy. He hated slavery and wanted to do something about it. In 1822, when he was about 53 years old, he organized a plan to take over the city of Charleston, South Carolina and the plantations that surrounded it. For months, he and his trusted friends planned the attack, but at the last moment, they were betrayed. This meant death for Vesey and his friends, one of whom went to the *gallows* saying, "Fear not, the Lord God that delivered Daniel is able to deliver us."

Nat Turner saw himself as a *prophet* for the deliverance of his fellow slaves. In 1831 he organized a rebellion around Southampton, Virginia. Turner and his followers went from plantation to plantation, killing whites regardless of age or sex. In the end, 60 whites were killed, but Turner was caught. After he was killed, whites became even more fearful of blacks. They *banned* any group activities and ruthlessly put to death anyone remotely associated with Turner. As one man stated, "The message was clear: America was home to the free, but only if you were white."

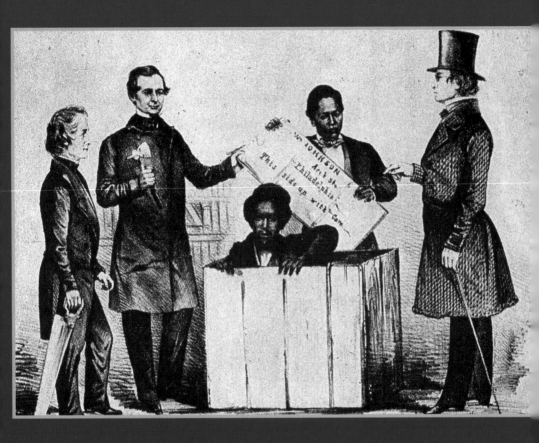

A black slave named Henry Brown came up with a clever plan to escape his plantation near Richmond, Virginia. He packed himself into a three-foot square wooden box, addressed to the Anti-Slavery Office in Philadelphia. The box was taken by mail carrier to the office, a trip that took 26 hours. After the package arrived in Philadelphia, abolitionists helped smuggle "Box" Brown over the border into Canada, where he would be safe.

cotton gin, a machine that efficiently removed the seeds from the cotton, made it possible to grow large crops to meet the demands of the *textile* industry in North America and England. By this time, importing slaves from Africa had been outlawed, but the slave population in North America was growing rapidly because the children of slaves became slaves themselves. By 1860 the slave population numbered four million, and at times the black population was equal to or greater than the white population in some areas. While an average of 100 slaves lived on tobacco plantations, a cotton plantation required 500 or more slaves.

With so many African Americans, why did they not revolt against the whites? This did occur occasionally, but for the most part, the slave population was separated by too much distance to be organized well enough to effectively overthrow their white owners. In addition, the whites controlled all the weapons, the horses, the money supply, and the local government. Laws prohibited slaves from gathering together in groups, from owning property, and from testifying against whites in court. If a slave rebelled or ran away, he or she was brutally beaten and sometimes killed to show others what would happen to them if they tried to be free. ✹

Harriet Tubman was born a slave around 1820 on a plantation in Maryland. She ran away to the North in 1849 because she was afraid she would be sold farther south. From 1850 until the start of the Civil War, she made 19 trips back to the South to lead slaves to freedom, using the abolitionist network known as the Underground Railroad.

# 5 The Road to Freedom

The cotton gin, large amounts of fertile land, and huge demand for cloth promoted the expansion of slavery. Growing cotton was big business, especially in the "lower" south, which included the states of South Carolina, Mississippi, Alabama, and Georgia. When the international slave trade was outlawed in North America, conditions actually improved somewhat. Slave owners began to realize that they needed to treat the slaves better than they had. Although the work was still long and difficult, and any time a slave broke a rule it meant severe punishment, owners encouraged family life and provided an improved diet and living conditions.

Overall, however, black slavery, with all of its terror, continued. This meant slave marriages were not legally recognized, a slave could not own property or earn wages, and a runaway slave was subject to death. As prosperity for whites grew and the contrast between them and slaves became increasingly apparent, *justification* for slavery began to emerge, especially in the South, where the way of life was based on slavery. Whites denied the humanity of African Americans. They said they were not ready for freedom because they were immature and would not work without being forced. Some said the black race was cursed and that God's punishment was slavery. Others called slavery a "necessary evil" and something that was actually good because it taught blacks about working and business.

As the United States came closer to Civil War, the turmoil over slavery grew. New states were entering the Union, and this posed the question of whether they were to allow slavery or not. A series of compromises in the federal government averted open conflict. In 1820, the Missouri Compromise outlawed slavery in lands north of Missouri. (This law was later overturned by the Kansas-Nebraska Act, which allowed people living in new states to decide for themselves whether or not they would allow slavery.) The Compromise of 1850 allowed California into the Union as a free state and outlawed slavery in the District of Columbia. However, this compromise also included the Fugitive Slave Act, which paid people for returning slaves to their owners. This created slave hunters who hunted down slaves in order to make money. Free blacks living in the north were now more insecure than ever. Many moved to Canada as a result.

As the controversy continued, there seemed to be some hope on the horizon. More people were speaking out against slavery. *Abolitionist* societies formed (although most did not include blacks as group leaders), and people like Harriet Tubman and Frederick Douglass courageously helped hundreds of fugitive slaves escape to Canada. "Colonizationists" felt it was best to return to Africa and start new countries, but most blacks did not feel this way. They felt the countries of North America were their homes, built with their labor, and that the laws of freedom and equality were for everyone, regardless of skin color. Abraham Lincoln often spoke in favor of abolishing slavery. He wanted to free blacks gradually and pay their

# CAUTION!!

## COLORED PEOPLE

### OF BOSTON, ONE & ALL,

You are hereby respectfully CAUTIONED and advised, to avoid conversing with the

## Watchmen and Police Officers of Boston,

For since the recent ORDER OF THE MAYOR & ALDERMEN, they are empowered to act as

# KIDNAPPERS

## AND

# Slave Catchers,

And they have already been actually employed in KIDNAPPING, CATCHING, AND KEEPING SLAVES. Therefore, if you value your LIBERTY, and the *Welfare of the Fugitives* among you, *Shun* them in every possible manner, as so many *HOUNDS* on the track of the most unfortunate of your race.

## Keep a Sharp Look Out for KIDNAPPERS, and have TOP EYE open.

*APRIL 24, 1851.*

An abolitionist poster warns blacks not to speak with "Watchmen and Police Officers," as they have been empowered to act as "kidnappers and slave catchers." Many blacks who escaped the South hid in Northern cities like Boston and Philadelphia, as these were centers of abolitionist activity.

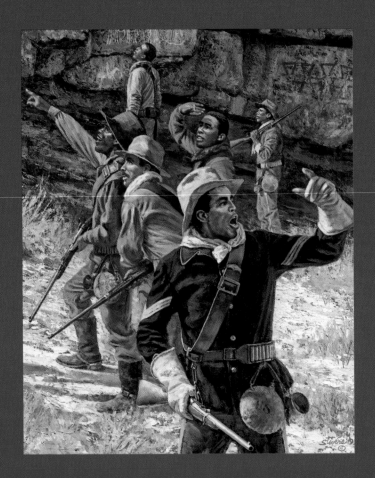

After the Civil War, newly freed blacks hoped to assimilate into the larger American culture. While many became farmers or laborers, some joined the U.S. Army. Two cavalry units and two infantry units made up of African Americans were created and sent to the frontier to fight Native Americans. They soon earned the respect of their opponents, who called the black troopers "buffalo soldiers."

owners for the loss of their slaves. In 1860, Lincoln was elected president of the United States. With Lincoln as president, the Southern states felt their cause was hopeless. They voted to leave the Union. First South Carolina **seceded**, then Mississippi, followed by Florida, Alabama, Georgia, Louisiana, Texas, Virginia, North Carolina, Arkansas, and Tennessee. These states became the Confederate States of America. When the Confederates attacked Fort Sumter in South Carolina, the United and the Confederate States of America were at war.

During the first two years of the American Civil War, Lincoln often stated that the cause for the fighting was to keep the Union together. But as the war continued, many urged him to add the elimination of slavery to this cause. During the fighting, some slaves stayed on their plantations, but others went over to the Union lines. Alfred Thomas was one of them. He said, "We had been hearing the guns...all over the country and everybody was scared and kept hearing people say the Negroes would be free and we heard colored people running off to the Yankees." About 180,000 African Americans eventually enlisted in the Union Army. Twenty-nine thousand joined the Union Navy. The army paid African-American soldiers less money than white soldiers received. Also, blacks were not allowed to become officers.

In September 1862, President Lincoln issued the Emancipation Proclamation, which freed slaves in the rebellious states. When Union soldiers went to the slaves on the plantations and announced their freedom, the African Americans were extremely joyful. Harry

Bridges recalled when the soldiers rode onto the plantation where he was a slave as a boy. When they told some of the women, they "rushed to [their] quarters telling the news to the other women and children." One woman was unable to believe she was free; it surprised her when the soldiers said she could leave the plantation if she wished and come and go as she pleased.

The United States government passed **amendments** to the United States Constitution granting basic rights to African Americans. The 13th Amendment abolished slavery in the United States. The 14th Amendment granted citizenship to all freed people, and the 15th Amendment gave African-American men the right to vote. (Black women, like other American women, were not granted this basic right until 1924.)

When freedom came for African Americans, former slaveholders and many Southern whites refused to recognize it. After the war, whites in local and state governments created laws, called Black Codes, that restricted the freedom of African Americans. For instance, blacks had to prove they worked for white people in many Southern states. Mississippi passed laws that prevented blacks from owning guns and from renting land in rural areas. Other states did not allow **interracial** marriages, prevented blacks from serving on juries, and stopped African Americans from testifying as witnesses in court against white people. White **vigilante** groups like the Ku Klux Klan also appeared. The members of these groups attacked blacks who had joined the Republican Party, which favored reforms. They also attacked black landowners and sympathetic whites.

For much of their time in America, people of African descent have had to contend with prejudice and hatred. While groups like the Ku Klux Klan are overtly racist, U.S. laws and policies have been discriminatory as well, treating blacks as second-class citizens.

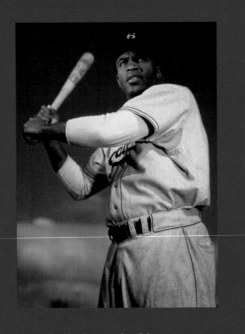

Baseball player Jackie Robinson was the first African American to play in the major leagues. He starred for 10 years with the Brooklyn Dodgers, and was elected to the Hall of Fame.

It was obvious African Americans still had to fight for their newly won freedom. But they were now paid for their work, and they could buy their own food, clothing, and shelter. And, blacks could live where they wanted to live and could travel freely. Freedom also meant education for black children. After the war, blacks became active in government. Over 600 African Americans became state legislators, and the people elected 16 African Americans to the United States Congress.

Freedom did not change some things, however. Many worked at the same jobs they had done when they were slaves. In the South, most still worked in the fields growing cotton, rice, sugar cane, and other crops. If one was a bricklayer or a blacksmith as a slave, he or she usually continued in that trade. In the workplace, African Americans faced *discrimination*. White employers often refused to hire them because they feared their white workers would not work alongside them. White workers also feared competition from newly freed blacks and would not allow blacks to join unions. Other labor practices limited black employment. Blacks were often paid less money for the same work that white workers performed. White employers often unfairly *fined* them for missing work and paid many former slaves only once a year. Because many were unskilled, blacks often performed work like shoveling coal, building roads, and digging ditches. Women were domestics or washwomen. An effort was made to include former slaves in the government workforce, where some became postal workers, customs workers, and deputy sheriffs. African Americans also took advantage of the Homestead Act of 1862 in which the U.S. government gave 160 acres to anyone who wanted to farm vacant land. In the west, blacks became soldiers, cattlemen, and cooks.

The "Jim Crow" laws of the 1920s and 1930s further restricted freedom for African Americans. These "separate but equal" laws, upheld by the United States Supreme Court, stated that separate facilities, like restrooms, and areas in hotels, restaurants, and public transportation could exist as long as they were of equal quality. Jim Crow laws allowed whites to promote the idea of separateness and inequality even though African Americans in theory were free. During the 1950s and 1960s, it would take a series of court orders, riots, and demonstrations to help remove legal obstacles to African-American freedom. The fight to provide the full benefits of citizenship to African Americans in the United States became known as the Civil Rights Movement.

Today, African Americans make up approximately 12.5 percent of the population of the United States. The 2006 American Community Survey, a project of the U.S. Census Bureau, estimates that there are more than 38 million black Americans, while another two million identified themselves as both black and another race.

Although the African-American population is growing, new black immigrants are not arriving as fast as immigrants of other ethnic backgrounds. By the year 2050, the African-American population is projected to increase to 15.7 percent of the total U.S. population, while the percentage of white Americans drops from about 70 percent of the total to 52.5 percent. The percentages of Hispanics and Asians in the United States will make up the difference, as there are greater numbers of immigrants arriving from these two groups than there are black immigrants.

In Canada, recent studies have set the number of African Canadians at more than half a million (about 2 percent of the total population). Although about 50,000 are descendants of escaped slaves or early settlers of Canada, the great majority of blacks arrived in the country during the past 25 years. The city of Toronto is home to a very large black community, estimated at nearly 250,000 people, while Montreal's African-Canadian community has more than 100,000 members.

African Americans have made important contributions to the development of society in North America. Although the African men and women brought as slaves in chains during the 17th and 18th centuries were unwilling immigrants, their descendants have created a place for themselves in the United States and Canada.

When Rosa Parks (right) refused to give up her seat on a bus to a white man in Montgomery, Alabama, she was arrested for breaking segregation laws. For the next year, African Americans in Montgomery refused to ride the buses until the company changed its policy of segregating black and white riders. The bus boycott, led by a young African-American minister named Martin Luther King Jr., was one of the first victories of the Civil Rights Movement.

# Chronology

**1502** Slavery is introduced in the West Indies.

**1617** San Lorenzo de los Negroes, a free town in Mexico for blacks, is established.

**1619** Twenty Africans arrive in the English settlement of Jamestown, Virginia.

**1700** Slavery becomes legal in the English colonies of Pennsylvania and Rhode Island.

**1708** African slaves are more numerous than Europeans in the colony of South Carolina.

**1776** The Declaration of Independence, proclaiming U.S. independence from England, states "all men are created equal."

**1787** The Constitution of the United States protects the institution of slavery.

**1793** The invention of the cotton gin helps promote the growth of slavery.

**1807** Foreign slaves are no longer allowed into the United States.

**1820** U.S. Congress passes the Missouri Compromise, which outlaws slavery north of the 36th parallel and allows Missouri to enter the Union as a slave state.

**1822** Denmark Vesey plans a revolt to take over Charleston, South Carolina, but is betrayed; he and his followers are put to death.

**1831** Nat Turner and 70 fellow slaves lead an uprising that leaves 60 whites dead; Turner and his followers are caught and hanged.

**1850** U.S. Congress passes the Compromise of 1850, which includes a harsh fugitive-slave law.

**1859** John Brown, a white abolitionist, leads slaves in a revolt on the U.S. arsenal at Harper's Ferry, Virginia; he is later caught and hanged; fear among slaveholders spreads.

**1860** Abraham Lincoln becomes President of the United States; seven southern states secede from the Union as a result.

**1861** The United States Civil War begins when Confederate troops fire on Fort Sumter in South Carolina; four additional Southern states join the Confederacy.

**1862** Lincoln issues the Emancipation Proclamation, freeing slaves in all territories in the South.

**1865** Civil War ends; Lincoln is assassinated.

**1890** Langston, Oklahoma, an all-black community, is founded.

**1896** U.S. Supreme Court rules that "separate but equal" segregation policies are constitutional.

**1910** The National Association for the Advancement of Colored People (NAACP) is founded.

**1945** World War II ends; one million African Americans have served in the United States armed forces during the conflict.

**1946** U.S. Supreme Court prohibits segregation on interstate buses.

**1947** Freedom rides test bus desegregation laws; Jackie Robinson becomes the first African American to play major baseball.

**1948** Segregation ends in the U.S. armed forces.

**1954** U.S. Supreme Court rules that school segregation is illegal.

**1955** A bus boycott begins in Montgomery, Alabama, after Rosa Parks is arrested for refusing to give up her seat to a white man.

**1957** Federal troops protect black students enrolling in a Little Rock, Arkansas, high school.

**1962** James Meridith becomes the first black to enroll in the University of Mississippi; riots erupt.

**1963** Governor George Wallace stands at the entryway to the University of Alabama to prevent a black student from enrolling; Martin Luther King Jr. leads 250,000 people on a march on Washington, D.C.; civil rights leader Medgar Evers is killed; President John F. Kennedy is assassinated; four African-American schoolgirls are killed in a church bombing in Birmingham, Alabama.

**1964** Martin Luther King Jr. receives the Nobel Peace Prize.

**1965** Malcolm X is killed in New York City; riots in the Watts section of Los Angeles leave 34 dead and $35 million in property damage.

**1967** Riots in U.S. cities leave many dead and neighborhoods in ruins; Thurgood Marshall becomes the first black U.S. Supreme Court justice.

**1968** Martin Luther King Jr. is assassinated in Memphis, Tennessee.

**1973** Tom Bradley is elected the first African-American mayor of Los Angeles.

**1977** More than 130 million watch the broadcast of the television miniseries *Roots.*

**1992** Four Los Angeles policemen are released after the beating of Rodney King; the riots that result are the largest and most costly in United States history.

**2001** Former U.S. Army general Colin Powell becomes Secretary of State in the administration of President George W. Bush.

**2008** The African-American population of the United States is estimated at more than 38 million.

## Famous African Americans

**Richard Allen,** 18th century religious leader and social activist

**Louis Armstrong,** jazz musician

**Benjamin Banneker,** scientist and mathematician

**James Beckwourth,** frontiersman

**Halle Berry,** Academy Award-winning actress

**Frederick Douglass,** abolitionist, writer, and orator

**Charles Drew,** physician

**W.E.B. Du Bois,** writer and sociologist

**Ralph Ellison,** author

**Medgar Evers,** civil rights leader

**Matthew Henson,** polar explorer

**Langston Hughes,** poet and critic

**Jesse Jackson,** civil rights leader and politician

**Martin Luther King Jr.,** civil rights leader

**Lewis Latimer,** scientist

**Malcolm X,** Black Muslim leader

**Thurgood Marshall,** justice of the U.S. Supreme Court

**Ronald McNair,** astronaut

**Barack Obama,** political leader

**Condoleeza Rice,** U.S. Secretary of State

**Sojourner Truth,** abolitionist and women's rights advocate

**Harriet Tubman,** abolitionist leader who helped guide many slaves to freedom

**Brooker T. Washington,** educator, author

**Ida B. Wells,** writer and orator

**Phillis Wheatley,** poet

## Glossary

**_Abolition_** to completely end slavery.

**_Amendment_** a proposed alteration or correction.

**_Artisan_** one who practices an art or craft.

**_Ban_** to prohibit by legal means.

**_Cannibal_** a person who eats human flesh.

**_Chattel_** personal property.

**_Calico_** printed cotton cloth.

**_Conflict_** a battle or fight.

**_Discrimination_** to show prejudice toward a person or group of people.

**_Emancipation_** the act of setting a person or a group of people free.

**_Fine_** to impose a monetary penalty.

**_Gallows_** a frame from which criminals are hanged.

**_Hereditary_** a condition that is passed down from an ancestor.

**_Hogshead_** a large barrel holding between 63 and 140 gallons.

**_Import_** to bring merchandise from one country into another country.

**_Indigo_** a blue dye obtained from certain plants.

**_Interracial_** between races.

**Justification** the act of defending an idea.

**Manacle** a shackle for the hand or wrist.

**Missionary** a person who travels to spread information about their religion to others.

**Moral** good or right in conduct or behavior.

**Overseer** one who directs or watches over the work of others.

**Prophet** a person who speaks for God as though under divine guidance.

**Secede** to formally separate from an organization.

**Servitude** a condition in which something owned by one person can be used by another.

**Steward** an employee on a ship, airplane, bus, or train who serves food and attends passengers.

**Tar and pitch** a black, sticky substance obtained from pine trees and used in ship maintenance.

**Textile** cloth.

**Vigilante** a person or group that acts outside of the law because of a perceived failure of the usual law-enforcement agencies.

**Wheelwright** a person who constructs and maintains wheeled vehicles, like wagons.

## Further Reading

**About the African Americans**

Barnett, Tracy. *The Buffalo Soldiers*. Philadelphia: Mason Crest Publishers, 2003.

Bennett, Jr., Lerone. *Before the Mayflower: A History of the Negro in America 1619–1962*. Chicago: Johnson Publishing Company, Inc., 1962.

Foner, Philip S. *History of Black Americans; From the Emergence of the Cotton Kingdom to the Eve of the Compromise of 1850*. Westport: Greenwood Press, 1983.

Herskovits, Melville J. *The Myth of the Negro Past*. Boston: Beacon Press, 1958.

Johnson, Charles and Patricia Smith. *Africans in America: America's Journey through Slavery*. New York: Harcourt Brace & Company, 1998.

Piersen, William Dillon. *Black Legacy: America's Hidden Heritage*. Amherst: The University of Massachusetts Press, 1993.

Young, Mary, and Gerald Horne. *To Make Our World Anew—A History of African Americans*. Robin D. G. Kelley and Earl Lewis, Eds. New York: Oxford University Press, 2000.

**Finding your African American ancestors**

Carmack, Sharon DeBartolo. *A Geneaologist's Guide to Discovering Your Immigrant and Ethnic Ancestors*. Cincinnati: Betterway Books, 2000.

Thackery, David T. *Tracking Your African-American Family History*. Salt Lake City: Ancestry, Inc., 1999.

Woodtor, Dee Parmer. *Finding a Place Called Home: A Guide to African-American Genealogy and Historical Identity*. New York: Random House, 1999.

## Internet Resources

**http://www.census.gov**

The official Web site of the U.S. Bureau of the Census contains information about the most recent census taken in 2000.

**http://www12.statcan.ca/english/census/index.cfm**

The Web site for Canada's Bureau of Statistics, which includes population information updated for the most recent census in May 2006.

**http://www.africanamericans.com/**

This Web site explores a variety of topics, including the history of African Americans, the Civil Rights Movement, slavery, African American art and more.

**http://afroamcivilwar.org**

The official Web site of the African American Civil War Freedom Foundation and Museum.

**http://www.history.org/Almanack/people/african/aahdr.cfm**

This page on the Colonial Williamsburg Foundation's official Web site discusses the life of colonial African Americans.

**http://www.nps.gov/revwar/about_the_revolution/**
**african_americans.html**

This National Park Service site examines the participation of African Americans in the Revolutionary War.

# Index

## Photo Credits

**Barry Moreno** has been librarian and historian at the Ellis Island Immigration Museum and the Statue of Liberty National Monument since 1988. He is the author of *The Statue of Liberty Encyclopedia*, which was published by Simon & Schuster in October 2000.
He is a native of Los Angeles, California. After graduation from California State University at Los Angeles, where he earned a degree in history, he joined the National Park Service as a seasonal park ranger at the Statue of Liberty; he eventually became the monument's librarian. In his spare time, Barry enjoys reading, writing, and studying foreign languages and grammar. His biography has been included in *Who's Who Among Hispanic Americans*, *The Directory of National Park Service Historians*, *Who's Who in America*, and *The Directory of American Scholars*.

**Richard Bowen** is a Wisconsin author whose books include *The Art of Hearing: Seven Practical Methods for Improving Your Hearing*, *Meeting Your Match—His Story*, and *Spirit and Nature*, a book of verse. He is co-owner of Ariadne Publishers and editor of the "Spiritual Awakenings" quarterly.